Dead Girl Walking

What's in a name...

Dr. AudreyAnn C. Moses

OTHER BOOKS BY DR. MOSES

Dead Girl Walking...
New Renaissance: A Collection of African American Fiction
(2022)
Edited by: Dr. Rhonda Lawson
Meet The World Image Solutions

Kelly Crews Publishing
The Heart Abound Novelette Series
The Swing (2018) (Book 1)

Earl Grey Chronicles
Uninvited Memories (2018) (Book 1)
A State of Affairs: Deception (2022) (Book 2)

Saved By Grace Series
Saved by Grace: Walking Through Affliction Into God's
Deliverance (2017) (Book 1)
The Story of Wade...The Road from Darkness to Redemption
(2020) (Book 2)

Voice of Truth Publishing

RITES OF PASSAGE:
Does It Give American Black Youths the "Right To Pass?"
(2010)
(Assisted by Kenneth Nyamayaro Mufuka, Ph.D.)

Acknowledgments

I just want to say Thank You God for helping me through some tough times and showing me that I am enough. Thank you to everyone willing to show love and compassion to another human just because.

Thank you to those who kept me encouraged.

To God be the Glory.

Dedication

This book is dedicated to every human who feels they are not enough. I pray Jane's journey helps you realize you are more than enough regardless of where you were born, how you were born, what you were called, or how you were treated. God loves you and He has a plan for your life. Stop permitting humans to steal your joy. Permit Him to show you how marvelous you really are.

"Blessed are the meek for they shall inherit the earth,"

(Matthew 5:5 KJV)

Contents

CHAPTER 1

Names...

Sometimes I wonder about the thoughts going through the minds of parents when they are naming their children. Do they name kids after great-grandma or grandpa because they want to honor their ancestors? Or, do they name their precious babies to declare their allegiance to or represent some worldwide or political cause? Or by the time they get to the last child, they have run out of ideas and just name them something they saw in a commercial or a magazine.

Every day I stand in front of my class preparing to call attendance and pray God help me pronounce the names of the girls in my class whose names all begin with "Me or Mi" and end with "sha, shea, or shia", with who knows what combination of letters in between. My Ph.D. is in Psychology, not Mythology. Only God knows why they put these combinations of letters together and how to pronounce them. Do parents not realize how important names are to the human spirit and that their child's name will make or break their entire life?

Let me tell you a story of a client who had such a name, She was referred to me by her social worker at the New Orleans Department of Social Services.

The year is 1989. The December weather is normally quite mild in New Orleans. There may be one or two cold weeks however, for the most part, winters were pleasant. This particular day was beautiful. Everyone was out running errands getting ready for the holiday season, eating beignets, drinking hot mochas for breakfast, and basically enjoying life.

Well, all except for one terrified young lady trying to save her life. In the tiny house she lives in on the West Bank in Gretna, LA, she is, once again, attempting to shield herself from another blow from her drunk at nine a.m. in the morning, trifling and very abusive husband. Unbeknownst to her this was the last straw for her neighbor who called the police and the Department of Social Services.

With her permission, I am telling her story. All names, except hers, are changed to protect the innocent and the guilty. Her name is Mrs. Janedoah Smith Burton and this is her story.

CHAPTER 2

Session #1: JEEZ-ZAS ... another one...

~~~

(Mrs. Janedoah Smith Burton is sitting in my office, with a black eye, a broken arm, and a two-year-old child clinging to her neck.)

"Hello, Mrs. Burton. My name is Dr. Roxanne Matthews. How are you feeling? Could I get you something to drink, coffee, water?"

"No ma'am. I'm fine."

"I am a Christian Life Coach. My specialty is personal growth and transition. It basically means I help people make positive changes in their lives if that is something they want to do. Is that something you may be interested in?"

"Maybe ... I guess so ... I don't know."

"Don't worry, most of us are not sure which direction is the right one to take, especially after dealing with the type of trauma you have had to overcome. As a Christian Life

Coach, I will help you find the course you feel would be right for you and your child. What we discuss is between you and me unless you decide to tell someone or give me written permission to do so. We have childcare here to help take care of your baby while we talk. They will be right here in the next room and you can look in on her as much as you need to. Is that okay?"

"Yes ma'am, that's okay."

"So, we can start by telling me why you were referred to me today?"

(Quite agitated) "I'm sure the social worker already told you, but I guess you want my words, right?!.

"Yes please."

"I have this neighbor who walks around passing out her Jesus papers and being nosey. Anyway, one night I ended up going to her house for help. I asked her if me and my baby could come to her house for a little bit. It was cold and raining and my husband had locked the door and I didn't have a key because my purse was in the house. She let me in, but I could tell she was turning her nose up at me in her head. I guess she remembered she is always leaving her Jesus papers on everybody's door and how would it look for her claiming to be a Christian while she is rolling her eyes and turning up her nose at me and my baby. You know what I mean, Dr. Matthews?"

I smiled, "Yes ma'am I know what you mean. So if I might ask, why did your husband lock the door with you and your baby still outside?"

(With an embarrassing smile) "He was drunk. He's always drunk. He is the same age as me, but he acts like an old geezer drunk, like he is 40 or something."

(I'm sure I raised an eyebrow at the thought of 40 being identified as old and geezer)

"Makes me sick. It's not my fault he got hurt and didn't go to college to play soccer. It's not my fault. It's his fault, he lost his scholarship. Then I got pregnant and he married me. So neither of us went to college. I didn't tell him to marry me. He said he was gonna marry me and take care of me and the baby proper like. My momma was glad because she already had a bunch of grandchildren running around because my trifling sisters and brothers don't take care of their own children. That's not my fault either. Nobody told my momma and daddy to have eight children and 59 grandchildren. Nobody. What were they thinking that they were only gonna have eight grandchildren? NOT! All of them, except one, have three or four kids. I'm not having no eight children...I can tell you that RIGHT NOW!"

(Mercy, I was praying my outside face wasn't repeating what my inside voice was saying...Mercy Me!)

"Anyway, he locked me out because he wanted chicken for dinner when he got home from work and I made meatloaf 'cause that's all we had. He was screaming and pacing the floor like the naked man in the caves Jesus had to heal. You know who I'm talking about, right? Mrs. Johnnes, that's my neighbor, gave me a paper about him and about how Jesus can heal crazy people. Well, I wish he was here now to heal my crazy husband! Anyway, I went outside to get away from him and calm down the baby and he locked the door and wouldn't let me back in. That's how I got locked out and ended up at Mrs. Johnnes' house that day. It was just by luck I had my phone in my pocket. He eventually called and said to come in the house, like he had no clue why I was out there in the first place. Crazy, don't you think?"

"I don't have a job right now. He is always blaming me for something dealing with money. I told him that just because I don't have a job someplace doesn't mean I don't take care of things around the house. Also, because I don't work, we don't have to pay for daycare. Do you know what he said to me? (*Eyes closed heavy sigh*) I'm trying not to cuss in your office Dr. Matthews, since you are a Christian and all. He said I would be paying for daycare out of my paycheck because **I** was the one who got pregnant. (*Another heavy sigh*) Can you believe that mess? Like he wasn't there inside me like a jackhammer having a spasm! (*She was not smiling, so, I did not smile*). Anyway, after he said that, he stormed out the door cussing, like he always does, and drove down the street. I sat there for about an hour fuming and crying because how could he say such a thing and think it was alright? How would he act like I got myself pregnant and this baby is not his responsibility too!"

"As it got on towards dark, I realized that he would be coming in drunk, cussing and hitting on me, and then try to make me have sex with him again. Dr. Matthews, have you ever had sex with a drunk? Disgusting! Anyway, I knew what I had to do and fast! So I packed a few things for me and the baby and I called my sister to come get me, but she wouldn't cause she has another boyfriend and he is sleeping over there. I knew I couldn't call my momma with all of her grandchildren running around. So, I did the next best thing. I went to Mrs. Johnnes house again. It was dark by now and I was afraid he was gonna see me before she came to the door. I banged on that door FOREVER. Finally, she came to the door looking like she was sleep. Who goes to sleep at 8:00 in the evening?! Christians I guess? They don't have much else to do. Anyway, she clearly didn't want to let me in, but she did and she let me stay there for about three days."

"You know what, Dr. Matthews, I was hoping he would not come home because he had been hit by a car or shot by another drunk in a bar someplace. Unfortunately, neither happened and the same day I decided it was safe to go home and get a change of clothes, he showed up claiming he had been all over the place frantically looking for me. He is such a liar. He had not been looking for me because if he was, Mrs. Johnnes would have been the first place he looked. Anyway, I knew he was at the bar every night, and I guess at work during the day. I never understood how those shipyard people could allow a stone-cold drunk to work on those ships every day. I'm surprised they did not fall apart as soon as they turned the darn things on."

"Anyway, he started acting like he was so sorry, like he always does. Then one thing led to another and we ended up in bed, well not physically in the bed. We were still in the front room, on the couch. The first time I just let him, the second time I said no because I had to go back to Mrs. Johnnes house and get the baby. He got mad and started beating me and throwing me all over the place and pulling my hair and..."

(Now she is clearly distraught, crying and pacing the floor. It is clear these were not love-hurt tears. These were angry, why-didn't-someone-shoot-him-in-the-bar tears.)

"I don't know what made Mrs. Johnnes come to the house, but I'm glad she did. I'm not mad she called the police. He would have killed me if she had not called for help. I'm so glad I left my baby with her. Who knows what he would have done to her?"

"Mrs. Burton, do you feel you have someplace safe to stay for the next few days? We can make arrangements for you and your baby if needed."

"I'm good, thank you. I will stay in my house or by Mrs. Johnnes since he is locked up."

"Dr. Matthews, I thank you for listening. No one ever listens to me...never. Other than my baby and Mrs. Johnnes, nobody cares about me either."

"Call me if you need me. Have a great evening."

"Yes ma'am. Thank you."

(Her session time was over but I allowed her to sit for a few minutes to calm down. I would have continued the session a little longer, but I had another client waiting and Mrs. Johnnes was waiting for her in the lobby. With her husband in jail, she was safe, for now. I scheduled her next appointment, gave her my card, and told her I look forward to seeing her on our next visit.)

CHAPTER 3

Session 2: Who is Janedoah Smith Burton?

⮑◦

(Mrs. Burton came to my office today for our second session. She looked rested. Her bruises were healing nicely. Of course, she was still in a cast. She did not have her baby with her today.)

"Good morning Mrs. Burton, how are you doing?"

"Good morning Dr. Matthews, I'm fine, how are you?"

"I'm fine thank you."

"I took your advice and got some rest. I'm grateful to Mrs. Johnnes for helping with Ruth, that's my baby girl's name, Ruth. I named her Ruth because it is such a calming name. He was going to name her Hazel, but I said no because there was a girl in high school named Hazel. She was horrible. She was a bully and she got along a little bit too well with the boys if you ask me. Even my husband, who was my boyfriend at the time, knew her well. I should have taken the hint and left him then. I was so stupid for love. If I knew then what I know now I would have left him a long time ago. Anyway, I did not want my child's name associated with the likes of her."

"Do you know how important it is to name your children the right kinda name, Dr. Matthews? A name sticks with you for the rest of your life. 'Bout the only good thing I got out of this marriage was I changed my last name. Thank God for that, since there is very little I can do about my first name."

"Why do you think a name is so important?"

"I know you are not going to say anything because you are so nice, but you know I have a ridiculous name. *(Shaking her head)* What were my parents thinking, you ask? They weren't thinking and they didn't mind telling me they weren't thinking."

"My invisible life began on December 5, 1969, in Biloxi, Mississippi. My parents already had seven other children, four boys, and three girls. Two sisters are twins. How could they have run out of girl names that quickly? I'm sure if they weren't just plain lazy they could have come up with a decent name for me. Well, obviously, that didn't happen."

"Like I said, we lived in Biloxi, Mississippi. We were dirt poor and I was the last thing on earth my parents or siblings wanted to see. And...(*a long pause and sigh*) and they treated me as such. You know that story about Cinderella, well, she was treated like a princess compared to me. It's my parents' fault. Why would you name a child Janedoah and pronounce it 'Jane Doe' just like a dead girl no one wants to claim? And then to top it all off, my last name was Smith! So basically, my name was the name of an unidentifiable dead girl!"

(*I could see tears welling in her eyes, so I asked her if she wanted a break, some water, or coffee. She said no and continued.*)

"When I was old enough to understand I asked my momma why did she do that to me...why did she name me something that would cause me to be teased and bullied all the time...even by my own siblings. She looked me in the eye and said what difference did it make what my name was and that I should be glad she named me anything because she did not want any more children and she would have aborted me if it wasn't a sin. That was the day I knew I did not matter to anyone on this earth. I was eleven."

(It bothered me she did not cry as she told me this. When it comes to her mother, it seems her spirit is numb. This is disheartening and may explain some of her decisions.)

"Mrs. Burton, how did you combat the bullying and teasing, especially from your siblings?"

"When I was little it used to hurt my feelings because I didn't know why nobody loved me. I figured it all out when one of my brothers told me I was as ugly as my name and that I wasn't his real sister. He treated me the worst. In school, I learned about birth order and that's when I realized he was jealous because he was no longer the youngest. But you know what Mrs., I mean Dr. Matthews, I don't know why he had his shorts in a wad all the time because he was still treated like the youngest and I was still treated like a straggler that wandered into the house and forgot to leave."

"What about your father?"

"What about him? He went to work, came home, got drunk, went to sleep, and did the same thing the next day until he died from ptomaine poison because he fell in the barn drunk and scraped his arm on a rusty nail and never went to the doctor. That was the only time I felt sorry for my momma. I remember her begging him to go to the doctor and he kept saying with what money. He would wash it with peroxide and tie an old rag around it. Next thing we knew he was too sick to do anything. My mom had to call an ambulance. He died on the way to the hospital. The good thing, if you can say such a thing, was that I was fifteen. My brother was seventeen. Everybody else was grown already and having babies of their own. My daddy had no decent insurance except for $3000 from his job, and a $2000 insurance policy. They paid the insurance man every month for as long as I can remember, and all my momma got for her miserable life my dad was a lousy two thousand dollars.

"You know who else jerks my nerves? Funeral people. They are the biggest crooks on the face of the earth. They are worse than used car salesmen. They stand there smiling at you with their palms itching trying to take every dime you got. Me and my momma did not have a right kinda mother-daughter relationship, but I was glad I watched this show about how to keep the funeral people from stealing you blind. She knew my older sisters and brothers were not gonna help her bury him, so for some reason, she decided to listen to me. I told her she could cremate him. She didn't want to do that just in case he was going to hell and she didn't want him to be burned twice. And if he is going to heaven she didn't want him to smell like smoke when he got there. I just said okay and helped her pick out a nice, CHEAP casket and everything. They were not church folk so we had a graveside funeral and called it a day. She was able to keep some of the insurance money. The one smart thing he did that she did not know about was he had a third insurance policy that paid off the house. It would be a blessing if you could say such a thing when somebody dies. If I ever buy a house, I will definitely do that."

"Do you want to know what is not surprising? Within a month or so of my dad's funeral, my momma was back to treating me like the ugly duckling, while her trifling grown ...a...um...behind children were nickel and diming her trying to get every penny she had left. They were worse than the funeral people. I never asked her for a dime and she never gave me one. Now her precious children drop their precious little gremlins off at her house and don't come back for a week or two to get them while they are doing whatever it is they are doing.

"Why do you call them gremlins?"

With an obvious smirk on her face, "Did you see the movie? Don't you remember what happened to those cute little cuddly creatures when they got wet? They turned into demons! That's them...demons!"

"My twin sisters looked alike, but otherwise they were as far from identical as twins could get. One of them joined the Navy and never came back. Well, she did come back for Daddy's funeral. She brought her family. They flew in that morning and flew out that evening. The other twin had a baby when I was about ten. She went to buy a loaf of bread and some milk, left town, and never came back, not even for Daddy's funeral. She sent money or a color book or something every now and again for my nephew, but not enough to amount to much. Half the time we didn't know where she was. He's a preteen now, giving momma all kinds of hell. My momma never filed child support papers on her. What's the point now?"

"Mrs. Burton, you said earlier that your name caused you a lot of issues throughout your life. Would you explain what you meant?"

"Dr. Matthews, my name is Janedoah Smith. Even though she tried to spell it fancy, it is still JANE DOE SMITH. Everybody knows that Jane Doe is the name they give dead women with no identification and Smith is the name people use when they don't want anyone to find them; you know because there are a trillion Smiths in every city in the world."

"My mother made it clear neither she nor my dad wanted me, or I guess no other child after my brother. After that she maintained the necessities, food-shelter-clothing, and the clothing was hand-me-downs from anybody. I always wondered if they continued having sex after I popped up." *(This was the first time she actually laughed out loud. Progress)*

"I remember one time, in high school, I was asked if I wanted to be on the school float for Mardi Gras. I was so excited, until I found out, since my name was Janedoah, they wanted me to be a zombie – Dead Girl Walking. At first, I was devastated, then mad. I wanted so badly to tell them all where to stick that float. My teacher talked me into going through with it. She was always nice to me, even when I wasn't in her class. She said if I never got another chance to be on a Mardi Gras Float I would regret throwing away this opportunity to prove to myself that I could be an important part of something. I'm glad I participated because I had a lot of fun, even though I was asked because my name was Jane Doe and they needed a – Dead Girl Walking."

"I could tell you a lot of stories, but what difference does it make now? I learned a long time ago that people treated me the way they did because of my name, and I let them."

"Why did you let them?"

"Why not? What difference would it make? They were gonna talk about me regardless of how much I protested. My own parents and siblings did not protest on my behalf, why should I? They did not love me then and they do not love me now. Do you want to know how I know? Because when this happened to me *(she raised her cast arm)*, NOT ONE of them came to my rescue. When he would beat me, I would call them and half the time they wouldn't even answer the phone. Brothers are supposed to protect their sisters…not mine."

"So is the reason you are here today because you have allowed …"

"I'm tired of talking now. I've used a week's worth of words in the 45 minutes I've been sitting here. I have to go. I'm sure Mrs. Johnnes is ready to give me back my baby so she can go pass out her Jesus papers."

"Will you return for our next appointment?"

(She looked at me as if she was trying to see past my face to discern why I didn't already know the answer to that question.)

"I have to come back."

"Why?"

"Because you listen."

(I made her next appointment and wished her a good day. When she was gone, I collapsed into my chair, and I prayed because my spirit was overwhelmed with the pain she carried. I don't see how Jesus carried the pain of the entire world to the cross when I was struggling with the pain of one little girl. Jesus thank you for your strength because I need you to help me with Mrs. Janedoah Smith Burton.)

CHAPTER 4

Session 3: Tears of a Clown

(Janedoah rescheduled her appointment. I was concerned I had hit a raw nerve. Actually, I know I did. Fortunately, her willingness to continue her sessions speaks loudly of how much she wants to stop the pain in her spirit.)

"*Good morning Mrs. Burton. How have you been since we last met?*"

"I'm fine, thank you. I had a lot going on lately that I had to deal with. That's why I rescheduled my appointment."

"*Do you care to discuss any of what you have been going through?*"

"Some of it had to do with my husband. He is out of jail and I had to get a restraining order so that he would leave me alone. I didn't know he was getting out. I was hoping for a couple of months before they let him have a bond. I was sitting on the porch when the police came with him to get his things out of the house. Every time the police weren't looking he said something ugly to me. He took the car. I told them I needed the car, but it's in his name, so he took it. He used the house bill money for bail and so now the rent is due. The courts don't care where the money comes from. I had to try to find help to pay the rent and light bill. I won't be able to pay it next month, so I will more than likely have to move. I don't work, so I don't have any income. He took all of the money out of the bank. And I don't have anywhere to go. So I guess me and Ruth will be homeless. I don't know where he went and he obviously doesn't care that his daughter will be homeless. How could a human being be so trifling and so mean towards another human being? Especially one they claimed to love at one time. And especially his own child. But why should he be better than his people or mine."

"Mrs. Johnnes said I could stay with her a little while longer, but her kids are complaining about me being there, mooching off of her. I don't mooch off of her. I keep her house clean and she lets me stay there. That's not mooching. Anyway, I can't stay there too much longer without having to cuss out her grown kids. They are big-time businesspeople who claim to be Christians. They all think they are better than me. What a joke! But the worst one is her preacher son. She is so proud of him. Driving to her house in his Cadillac acting like he is God Himself. He about choked on his iced tea when I walked in the house and he saw me. Do you want to know why? He recognized me. Do you want to know why he recognized me? It would break Mrs. Johnne's heart to know that her preacher son is cheating on his wife in the hood with my girlfriend. So when they are not treating me like the maid they are trying to get rid of me, especially him. He is terrified I will "slip" and tell his mother about his girlfriend. He better worry she and I don't show up to his church in our Pretty Woman Sunday Hoochy-Mama Best, Big Hair included! I wanna see what kind of praying he'll be doing then! If I did not despise him so much I would laugh, but there is nothing worse than cheating men."

(I wanted to laugh, but she was serious so I prayed my inside thoughts were not showing on my face).

"They can treat me any way they want. Mrs. Johnnes' house is very big and she is getting up in age and can't keep it up the way she would like. Her kids don't come and help her. Her house needs repairs. Do you think either of them will call a plumber or an electrician? Nope! I guess it doesn't matter if you are rich or poor, your children can still be trifling. I'm thinking about asking her to hire me as her housekeeper full-time and maybe rent one of her rooms for me and Ruth. It will at least keep me on my feet until I can do better."

"Mrs. Burton ..."

"Please call me Jane. I want to be known as Jane Burton. Mrs. Johnnes calls me Jane and I like the way it makes me feel when I respond to that name. Jane is a name I can be happy with."

"Jane, I remember during our first session you said you were stuck with your first name forever. I'm glad to know you decided that was not the case."

"You have told me who Janedoah is and is not. You have told me how you allowed yourself to become that person. Who is Jane Burton? Where does she want to fit in the world?"

(I could see the moisture welling up in her eyes and her body tense)

"Why is that important? Why is it important for me to be able to tell you who I am…who I want to be? Why is that so important? I'm no different! I had dreams for my future. You see where that got me. Beat up and homeless."

"Until you can say who you are and what you really want out of life it will be difficult to find your true place in this world. God created all of us for specific reasons to touch the lives of specific people. Satan will deceive us by making us believe that others are correct in their misrepresentation of us. His goal is to have us believe the lie to the point that we cannot hear The Holy Spirit telling us who we really are, and more importantly, whose we really are. In your case, Satan enticed people to tell you that you were worthless because of your name. They believed his lie and you believed their lie."

"Dr. Matthews you sound like Mrs. Johnnes now. She is always talking about how God has a purpose for everyone. I told her the only reason I was born was so the world would have someone to mistreat. That's my purpose on this earth. She said no human born or waiting to be born was put on this earth to be mistreated. Satan decided it was his job to make as many people as possible as miserable as he was. She is always telling me to read something and that I have to affirm and decree that I am better than my name and my circumstances. I never grew up with people going to church and talking about God. I told you my momma said she didn't know if my daddy went to heaven or hell. He probably didn't know either until he got there."

"All I know about me is what I've been called all my life. Dead Girl Walking. Nobody ever talked nice to me. I'm not pretty, but at least somebody could have lied. *(Then she smiled)* Well, one person did. How do you think I ended up in the situation I'm in now? Remember I told you about the Mardi Gras Parade? Well, he was the only one that did not tease me. He said that even dressed and made up like a Zombie I was still pretty. I thought it was a trick for people to laugh at, so I told him to leave me alone. But he didn't. Every day at school, he would find me and tell me I was pretty or something. Eventually, I fell for it. We dated sophomore and senior years. I had planned to go to the community college and he had a scholarship to play soccer at a college."

"I told you he got hurt and lost his scholarship. He went to community college and learned how to be a mechanic. I wanted to go for Early Childhood Education but I got pregnant. Then we got married. Then I couldn't work because we could not afford daycare. When he got a raise I wanted to work at the elementary school as a teacher's aide. He said no he wanted me to stay home with Ruth."

"Things were going well for us until he got passed over for a promotion because he didn't have a bachelor's degree. I remember that day well because it was our second anniversary. I didn't have money for presents so I cooked his favorite food, fried chicken smothered in gravy with rice. He didn't come home that night or the next night. When he finally came home he said it was my fault he had to work double shifts to make ends meet and that he didn't get the promotion because he didn't finish college, which, of course, was my fault also. That's when he started drinking more and more, staying out more and more, and complaining more and more about the bills, about me, about Ruth, about everything."

"Then he started hitting me, mainly when he was drunk. At first, it was a slap or a shove or something, then he would apologize and make love to me. The next day he would bring flowers or something."

"What I didn't know before I married him was that his father drank and beat his mom on a regular basis until they both died in a car accident. He was driving drunk and ran the car off the side of the road. We were in high school when the accident happened, but I didn't know the details. He lived with his aunt and uncle until we got married. Out of the two and a half years we have been married, we have only had a few good months, if you add all of the good days together. He is broken and I am broken. A marriage made in hell."

"What do you want now...for yourself and Ruth?"

(She sat there for a couple of minutes in silence. Wiping her eyes a little bit. Staring at her hands. Not saying anything. As I waited, I prayed for peace in her spirit.)

"You asked me who am I. I don't know who the real Jane Burton is going to be. I've never met that person. What I do know is who I want the real me to be. I want to be the

Jane that can keep Ruth safe. I want to be the Jane that is happy to be alive. I want to be the Jane who can take care of herself and raise Ruth the opposite of how her father and I were raised. I want to be the Jane who believes it when people say she was put on the earth to help people, not to be hurt by people."

"Did I tell you why I named my baby Ruth? While I was pregnant, I read one of Mrs. Johnnes' Jesus papers that told the story of a girl named Ruth. I'm sure you know the story, being a Christian yourself and all. Anyway, to make a long story short, Ruth learned how to leave the muck of where she grew up and walked into a life of love, kindness, and happiness. She no longer had to smile so people wouldn't see her tears. That's what I want for Ruth. That's what I want for me. But, you and I both know that *that* Jane does not exist. She only lives behind my tears."

Jane looked at her watch, "I have to go now. I told Mrs. Johnnes I'd come straight back so she could run some errands. I told her I could bring Ruth with me, but she wouldn't have it. She has fallen in love with Ruth. Maybe she is Ruth's Naomi. Maybe she is my Naomi too."

"Thank you, Dr. Matthews."

"For what Jane?"

"Listening."

"You are welcome. And Jane..."

"Yes ma'am?"

"I will be praying that you find clarity and peace in your spirit."

"Thank you."

(When Jane left I again prayed for her. I prayed she found peace in her spirit, enough so she could hear The Holy Spirit talking to her. Peace enough so she can hear her voice and the voice of the Jane of her dreams and realize they are the same voice...hers.)

CHAPTER 5

Session 4: Timing is everything...

(The moment I saw Jane's face I knew something happened since our last session. She sat still as a board and would not look in my direction, not even when she spoke.)

"Jane, it's a nice day. How about we go for a walk? I've been cooped up in here all morning and could use some fresh air. Are you okay with walking while we talk?"

With an agitated look on her face, she said, "If that's what you need it's fine with me."

After a few moments of very silent walking, I asked, "Jane, what has happened? Did your husband violate the restraining order? Did he attack you again?"

"No ma'am he didn't. He didn't do anything. I just got a lot on my mind, that's all."

"I see. So, we can walk until you are ready to tell me what is on your mind."

She almost rolled her eyes at me and muttered, "You don't know how to live in silence for too long, do you Doc? I love the way you listen but that doesn't mean I want to talk all the time. Sometimes, it's too hard to say the words."

"Like now?"

"Yes...like now!"

(So we had a very brisk and very quiet walk around the block...twice. What was I thinking recommending a walk on what was the coldest day in the history of New Orleans!)

"Dr. Matthews. Something terrible has happened and I don't know what to do about it. If I tell the person that needs to know, I know the outcome will be devastating, especially for me. I'm just wondering if I should just worry about myself, I don't know what to do."

"If I'm understanding you correctly, if you tell it will cause trouble for you, and if you don't tell it will cause trouble for you. So, my question to you is who will get hurt most?"

(So we walked a little further in silence.)

"I'm pretty sure I am pregnant. Well, actually, I know I'm pregnant." *As she sat on the bench she started to cry,* "I missed my cycle last month. I just thought it was stress. When I missed it this month I knew it wasn't just stressed. I bought a test. I'm pregnant."

"I haven't spoken to my husband at all since he left. He has not returned my calls. To be honest, I don't want to tell him, because I don't want him to think he can come back, or worst that I got pregnant on purpose...even though he raped me...well, he didn't rape me but, you know what I mean. **WHAT** if he says it's not his...I swear to God I will catch a charge. Regardless, I am so done with him."

"I haven't told Mrs. Johnnes yet, although she is old and I'm sure she already knows I'm pregnant. You know how those old women are. All they have to do is look at you and they know. It's like there are pheromones for pregnant women that only the grandmothers can smell. You know what I mean?"

(Jane smiled even while she was shaking her head in disbelief.)

As we were finally entering my office, "So Jane, what did you mean when you said you don't know what you are going to do?"

"Did you forget I already have a baby and that we are homeless? How can I take care of two babies by myself? No education, no job, no house, no money, NO NOTHING!

I did think, for a second or three, about an abortion, but that's not my thing. It's not this baby's fault he or she has a jacked-up daddy and a momma with no means to take care of him or her. It's not the baby's fault. The baby deserves a chance to make the world a better place. I will not be trying to explain to God why I decided something he caused to have life didn't deserve to live. So no, I'm no longer considering an abortion. However, the fact that it did cross my mind is sad and disturbing in itself. Don't you think that shows just how unstable I am right now?"

(She started to cry again.) "Oh God, *what* am I supposed to do now? Mrs. Johnnes says You have all of the answers, so WHAT IS YOUR ANSWER TO THIS PIECE OF MESS!"

As I handed her a tissue box and a bottle of water, "Jane, you must tell Mrs. Johnnes. I'm sure she will be able to help you. Also, have you made a prenatal appointment yet? The sooner you do the sooner you will be able to get other prenatal services, including WIC which will help to keep you,

Ruth, and your baby on a healthy nutritional diet. If you are using WIC now for Ruth, they will increase it for you while you are pregnant and for the baby once he or she is born. I'll have my secretary help you make the necessary appointments."

"Thank you that would be fine. I already made a doctor's appointment at the free clinic. I go on Thursday. That's another reason I will have to tell Mrs. Johnnes. I'm gonna need her to watch Ruth if she's not busy."

Shaking her head again, "After I had Ruth and he started beating me I prayed not to get pregnant again because I knew I could figure out how to take care of me and Ruth by myself. I took precautions, but I guess God has a very warped sense of humor and other plans for me and Ruth."

"And your husband."

"If you say so. Right now I'd be okay if police came and told me he fell off of a cliff someplace."

"Jane, God don't like ugly. Also, you do know that you and your babies are going to be just fine. God has never and will never leave you or forget about you. Believe that."

Jane started to cry again, "Dr. Matthews, you say He won't ever leave me or forget about me, but God has been mad at me all of my life and my punishment has been all the trouble I've had to deal with. So why should this baby be any different? My entire life has been a disappointment for someone, including me. Mrs. Johnnes always says God don't make mistakes. I guess you believe the same thing...that God don't make mistakes. This baby, in His eyes, may not be a mistake, but when I can't feed it, someone is gonna say I made a mistake letting myself get pregnant. The only mistake I made was letting my husband inside of me. If I had not I'd be dead now for refusing him. The problem with that is Ruth would have lost the only family member who really loves her. One family member who truly loves you is all anyone ever really needs, don't you think?"

"Yes, I think. I also think when we are hurting we don't allow ourselves to believe that we actually deserve better than what we are used to. Because we have only experienced a life full of deceit, hurt, loss, and pain."

"*But God is a God of many chances. Everything about our lives is timed right down to the moment, So...*"

"So are you saying God orchestrated this mess I'm in on purpose? How is that possibly a good thing!"

"*It's important we understand God does not create mess, we do. The Bible says in 1 Corinthians 14:34, 'For God is not the author of confusion, but of peace...'. (I could see the pain on her face that was obviously in her spirit). At some point in our lives it is up to us to choose a life without confusion, or as you call it, mess. We have to understand there comes a time when we are in control of our destiny, and the only way we miss that timing is because we are so busy looking back we can't see where we should be going. Life is about timing, and God points us in the direction we should be going at the time we should be going there. It is our choices which point our feet in the right or wrong direction.*"

"Dr. Matthews, I guess you and Mrs. Johnnes have been talking to each other about me. Well, I'll ask you what I asked her...how am I supposed to make a choice when I don't even know how to get out of where I am now!" God has not shown me anything except grief."

(Jane stands to leave.)

"Before you leave let me give you something to think about. The day your husband locked you out of the house, how did you know to go to Mrs. Johnnes? How did you know you could go back to Mrs. Johnnes when you ran away? How did you know you would be able to trust me? And most importantly, why have you continued to come?"

"I don't want an answer from you now. When you are ready to answer, call and make an appointment. Okay?"

"Yes...I guess so if that's what you want."

"Jane..."

"Yes ma'am?"

"It's important that it be what you want. I'll see you next time."

"Yes ma'am."

(Before walking out of the door Jane hesitated. Her facial expression said she had no clue what her next step would be. I'm praying she will allow herself to hear God talking to her.)

CHAPTER 6

Session 5: Jesus is the Answer...

"Hello, Dr. Matthews how are you? Since it's been three weeks since I've been here I know you probably thought I wasn't coming back."

"Jane, I was happy to see you had made an appointment. I left it in the hands of the One I knew had all the answers."

"You and Mrs. Johnnes say that a lot. I told her about your questions. She added one. She asked me do I want to hear the truth about who I really was. Am I ready to agree I am forever God's child and God's children are not all of those ugly things people labeled me with all of those years."

"I see Mrs. Johnnes is trying to take my job, I'll have to start splitting my fee with her."

She laughed, "I thought your fee was free?"

"It is!"

We both had a good laugh. "So, what is your conclusion about the questions we asked you? How do they connect to your current situation?"

"Mrs. Johnnes house is about three doors down from where I lived but in the curve. She could literally look directly at my house from her front door. When he wouldn't unlock the door, I went to my two neighbors next to me. They were not at home. The other house is an old man that I don't trust. I never talk to him. So Mrs. Johnnes was the next available house. When he was drunk and beating me my family was always conveniently not available. There was no one else but Mrs. Johnnes. I just assume it was fate. Now that I have listened to her talk and your talk, I guess God was making sure I went to the right house. I came to you because my social worker told me to. I'm accustomed to doing what I'm told. She said you were safe, but the way you talk and the way you listen is why I let myself trust you and why I continue to come back. I came back because you listened. I know you want me to see 'God's handy work'... that's one of Mrs. Johnnes favorite sayings... 'God's handy work' in this... 'God's handy work' in that. I know you want me to see His handy work in my life, but I'm still struggling to understand if He loved me so much why did he allow all of those bad things to happen to me? If you love someone you are supposed to protect them, not hurt them. When I asked Mrs. Johnnes this questions, you know what she did, gave me one of her Jesus papers. She love her Jesus papers. This one was about Job. I guess his momma decided to call him Job to remind him to get a job. (*She had to laugh at herself after saying that*). Jokes aside, I asked her why would God allow Satan to do all of those terrible things to him. Why was Job used to prove a point? How is that love and what point is He trying to make with me?"

"She said the story teaches us that even though God knows Satan is gonna tempt us to do wrong and even hurt us into thinking God does not love us, it is our choice to choose God over Satan. She said that Satan's job is to kill, steal, and destroy, but God's job is to show us unconditional love. She showed me that scripture, John 10:10. You know it? The first half is Satan killing and destroying and the second half is Jesus giving people a better life. I told Mrs. Johnnes I wish I could get a better life. She said I could if I honestly believe that God would give it to me."

"It sounds as if you and she had a very serious bible study."

"Yes, I suppose we did."

"Well, I came here to tell you I'm ready to do the work."

"Work?"

"Yes, I'm ready to work on my relationship with me. Are you ready?".

CHAPTER 7

Session 6: The caterpillar has to die first...

(Jane and I have been working on some strategies to help her build her sense of self-worth, self-identity, and self-esteem. She has been making progress, slow but sure, especially in building her self-worth. She is realizing that she is worthy, even if no one else agrees. She is identifying immediate and long-term goals she would like to accomplish.

Today I noticed an immediate difference in Jane. Her hair was styled nicely. Usually, it's pulled back in a quick ponytail. No makeup but a little bit of lipstick, pearl earrings, and necklace. She had on a simple dress that fit her nicely with a pair of low-heel pumps. This time I wasn't able to keep my inside voice off of my face. She smiled.)

"" Hey there Dr Matthews, how are you doing?

"I'm well Jane, how are you doing?"

"Good. I guess you almost did not recognize me when I walked in. I read in one of those books you gave me that I have to look the part I want to achieve. So, that's what I plan to do from now on. Now mind you I did not throw away my jeans and things. I still like that look also, but when I'm conducting business, I want to look like a businesswoman, not like a neighborhood girl." *(She laughed. She's been laughing more lately...this is good)*

"Mrs. Johnnes told me that God gives me permission to move any mountains that are in my way. Do you know that scripture? Mark 11:22-25. She said mountains in this scripture could represent my obstacles. It says that if I tackle an obstacle in Jesus' name it has no choice but to dissolve. Satan can't live in the same house where Jesus lives. You know Mrs. Johnnes is gonna make sure I know Jesus is the answer to turn every frown I have into a smile. You were right when you said God sent me and Ruth to her house. I learned what has become my favorite praise song". *(Jane begins to sing)*...

"If you have some questions, in the corners of your mind.

And traces of discouragement and peace you cannot find.

Reflection of the old past, they seem to face you every day.

There's one thing I know for sure that Jesus is the way.

Jesus is the answer for the world today; above Him, there's no other Jesus is the way…"

"Jane I see there are a few talents you have been hiding, you have a beautiful voice. I hope you use it more often. And yes, I love Andrae' Crouch's music. He was one of my favorite gospel singers. Yes, that song is an affirmation of how to create a Jesus atmosphere around your life."

"Well, I'm doing something you are probably not going to like, being a Christian and all. *(She laughed again.)* I filed for a divorce. It will be final in a couple of months. I decided I would not live my life in fear of never being able to be more than what I was."

"You was?"

"Yes ma'am…I was. I have learned I am somebody special and I am worth more than I've been taught and treated like all of my life; and definitely worth more than a name."

"I have something else to tell you that might make you a little bit sad. It made Mrs. Johnnes very sad. *(Deep sigh)* I'm moving away. I called my sister who is in the Navy. She lives in Beaufort, SC. She will be retiring soon and she bought a house in Beaufort, not far from the water. She and I had a long talk. Do you know she said she always hated the way everyone treated me, like it was my fault I was born? She said it was not my fault, none of it. She said she was sorry for leaving me to deal with it all, but she had to leave in order to save her own life. She said if I wanted Ruth and I could come live with her and her family and I could have my baby there. She would help me get the proper services I need. They have an apartment over their garage they planned to rent out and I could rent it if I want. I could help take care of her boys and keep her house until I got a job and finished school."

"Beaufort? Finish School?"

(Big Smiles) "Yes Ma'am! I'm going to finish my degree and become a special education teacher. I know that I can make a difference for children who feel they have been

ostracized because they are different. What do you think
of that?"

*"Jane, that is a wonderful plan. I am so happy to have met
you and I'm honored you trusted me enough to assist you
along your journey. You have my card. Please keep in touch.
When do you leave?"*

"We leave in a few weeks. I have another doctor's
appointment and I have a few other things which still need
to be wrapped up. I have to pack out my little bit of stuff.
Mrs. Johnnes had labeled a bunch of stuff in her house to
be sent with Ruth and me. She also had started a nursery
for the baby. I told her she didn't have to do that but she
insisted. She said she would come to help me when I had
the baby. I'm sure her children will have a cow. She is
more my mother than my momma would ever be."

*"Have you spoken to your mother? Does she know you are
leaving? Does she know you are having another child? How
does she feel about it?"*

"I told her...she doesn't care. To be honest, I think she does
care but she doesn't know how to express it. All of her
favorite children still don't check in on her like she

thought they would. The only time she sees them is when they are dropping their kids off or coming to ask for money. They use her and she lets them. Even her favorite little boy. He does at least check on her and make sure she has what she needs, but he doesn't live there. She lives alone. She is alone. It's sad. I will try to keep up with her. Maybe I'll come back once in a while so that she can see my children, maybe."

"So, you still don't want to know the gender of your baby?"

She smiled, "No ma'am. I want it to be a real and happy surprise."

"What about your husband?"

"He's in jail again. He doesn't care about us either. When I get to Charleston I'll file for child support and let the state deal with him. I'm done. Maybe Mrs. Johnnes will send him some of her Jesus papers."

"Jane, do you remember when you first came to me you described yourself as a 'Dead Girl Walking'? Well, Mrs. Jane Burton, I am happy you no longer refer to yourself in such a way."

It has truly been a pleasure working with you and if you ever need to just talk, please call. If you need a personal recommendation I will be happy to write one for you. You continue to walk with your head high. The view from the balcony is lovely. Don't go back to the basement and don't leave any down there that you can help lift up...even your momma and, your husband. You be blessed and I know you will be a blessing to others.

I have this card I'd like you to keep with you. Read it whenever you need it."

If you want to become successful in life...

1. **Change your mindset: You don't get in life what you want, you get in life what you are.**

2. **Practice OQP: Only Quality People**

3. **Develop your communication skills because once you open your mouth you tell the world who you are.**

Les Brown

(Teary eyed), "Dr. Matthews?"

"Yes, Jane."

"Is it okay if I pray for you?"

Again, is my inside voice showing on my outside face, because now I'm in tears, "Yes, of course…always."

She reached out to hold my hands, "Mrs. Johnnes said it's always good to hold hands when possible."

She cleared her throat, "Our Father who are in heaven, hollowed be thy name. Thy kingdom come thy will be done on earth as it is in heaven. Give us this day our daily bread and forgive us our debts as we forgive our debtors. And lead us not into temptation but deliver us from evil. For thine is the kingdom, the power, and the glory forever, and ever…Amen." (Matthew 6:9-13).

(She stood for a moment before releasing my hands. I could not stop the tears, hers or mine.)

"Thank you Jane, that was a beautiful prayer."

"You are welcome, Dr. Matthews."

"Thank you, Dr. Matthews."

"For what Jane?"

"Listening."

Epilogue

Starting Over

Starting over, what will I face?
Will it be a fresh start in a new place?
Will it be new discoveries or a repeated past?
I need to slow down and not move so fast.
Am I starting with or without grace?
Lord, slow my feet and steady my pace.
My decisions are never my own.
Lord, guide me and usher me into a new home.
Starting over, what will I face?
It is a fresh start in a new place.
Lisa M. (Ferguson) Thompson
9/26/2023

****

Follow Jane as she discovers a new life and unfamiliar world for her young family in "Jane's Journey". Allow me the privilege of sending you event notices about Jane and my other books by providing your contact information at https://www.transitionlifecoach4u.com.

About the Author

Dr. AudreyAnn Moses is a Certified Christian Life Coach, Mental Wellness Counselor, and Best Selling Author (fiction and non-fiction). She is involved in several community-based programs focusing on personal and professional development and is an experienced workshop/program facilitator.

Dr. Moses has written books and articles and has conducted workshops on personal growth, self-care, and transition. She writes fiction novels addressing situations found in most families. Her stories focus on physical, mental, emotional, relationship, and spiritual trials. Her books are found on Amazon, Barnes and Noble (NOOK), Goodreads, and other venues where books are sold. For autographed copies contact Dr. Moses at (NeverSayCain't Christian Life Coach & Consultant - Order, Books (transitionlifecoach4u.com).

AudreyAnn and husband, Leonard, currently live in the quaint rural community of Cokesbury in Hodges, SC. They have four adult children, ten grandchildren, and one great-grandson which she feels qualifies her as a life coach and to write stories of Christian family dynamics, love, and devotion to each other and to God. Learn more about her coaching services and purchase her books by browsing her Linktr.ee link: https://linktr.ee/moses.ayann

www.ingramcontent.com/pod-product-compliance
Lightning Source LLC
Chambersburg PA
CBHW060428090426
42734CB00011B/2487